No More Regrets

Written By:
Prophetess Angela Horn

authorHOUSE®

AuthorHouse™
1663 Liberty Drive
Bloomington, IN 47403
www.authorhouse.com
Phone: 1-800-839-8640

Published by AuthorHouse 10/24/2014

ISBN: 978-1-4969-4274-6 (sc)
ISBN: 978-1-4969-4273-9 (e)

Preface

First and foremost, I love putting the Lord's divine purpose first in everything I do. Having been saved at the age of twenty-two, and being a single mother of three, I was—and am to this day—determined to fulfill God's purpose in life. I remain dedicated to helping families, children, men, and women to overcome crises that would have eventually destroyed them but instead brought them closer to the Lord. I have always had a heart for helping hurting people. My training and work experience have propelled me in my ability to help people in need. As a young woman, I began working as a residential homemaker assisting the elderly. I then began working with juveniles in the justice system. As God continued to move in my life, I later began counseling and assisting battered women and victims—both men and women—of alcohol and drugs.

It was in 1998 that I was called into ministry full time. God placed in my spirit the phrase "Women Standing in Liberty." What started out as a ministry for helping women turned out to help many women, men, and children, in the name of Jesus Christ, to find their true purpose in life. While healing minds from mental and physical abuse, helping them grow in the Lord, and preaching the Word of God with the wisdom and knowledge that God placed inside of me, I continued to be directed by the Lord.

I have helped people by using my own past experiences: healing from cancer, the death of a child, deaths of my mother and brother, persecutions, financial problems, and many other things that evil brings to this life here on earth. While still giving my testimony, despite all the major storms that were raging in my life, I continued to help others, even as I drew closer to God. I sought my own divine healing and watched God perform major miracles in my life and the lives of others. After the death of my son, God led me to Cottonwood, Alabama. I refused to give up on life and God. Obeying God, I went to Alabama to encourage other women and to help them get through their hurts and begin the healing process after the deaths of loved ones. Many women were set free from hurt and pain.

I've always believed and hold fast to these sayings: "I can't help anybody unless I've helped myself" and "The blind can't lead the blind."

In 2007, I became founder and president of Liberty Without Walls Ministries, Inc. Through a phenomenal prayer line, a church ministry was established. Since then, God has used, beyond belief, these ministries inside of me to touch many lives. He continues to do amazing miracles through me locally in my hometown community of Thomasville, Georgia, and also abroad through telephone conference calls. My ministry is truly designed with you in mind!

Contents

Introduction

Isaiah 26:7 in the Contemporary English Version says, "Our Lord, you always do right, and you make the path smooth for those who obey you."

This book is written for those who are sick and tired of living lives full of regret. You can have a complete turnaround in your life by reading this book and following the steps that God has for you to take. God can take you out of a dark path or dilemma that you have created and bring you into a life of success through the leading of his Word. God wants to change the way you think so that you can have everything he promised to give you. Everything that is written in his Word shall come to pass. God's word is so true! We just need to believe in him and hear the "I am" in our thoughts, which was the way he identified himself to Moses: "'But what should I say, if they ask me your name?' God said to Moses: I am the eternal God. So tell them that the Lord, whose name is 'I Am,' has sent you" (Exodus 3:13b–14 CEV).

If you believe what the Scripture says, you can change all of the crooked places in your life in an instant. You see, God never intended for us to make more mistakes and have less success. He will be whatever and whoever you want and need him to be. God wants us to have greater successes and fewer regrets. This book contains several stories about my life and how God took bad situations (negative) and became the "I Am" in my life (positive), blessing me to a place of good health, wealth, and prosperity.

1

Relationships

My story begins with me as I knew myself. I always wanted to be loved, cherished, and married. This was all I ever wanted, and I had it on my mind from the time I knew myself. I wanted this more than having dolls to play with.

All I ever wanted was a husband like my dad. He was such a loving husband to my mother and a very good dad to me and the rest of my twelve sisters and brothers. I never saw him hurt my mother in any way. He would always say to us that our mother was as pretty as a rose and that no one could ever compare to her. My mother said that she was spoiled because she knew that my dad truly loved her very much. And he did! He showed it every day in every part of their life together.

Every child, person, neighbor, family, or friend who ever knew my dad and mom could say the same.

When I looked at their life as a married couple, they made marriage seem so easy and desirable to me. Some people say they'll never get married because of the way they have seen their parents live or because siblings represent their marriages in a bad way. I never even thought about dating. I just wanted a life like my parents' life. I was born the fifth-youngest child out of thirteen children, and it never occurred to me to date someone to get to know him before getting married.

Looking back at the way I was thinking—or *not* thinking—I realize that this was why my life began to go downhill. I can see how this happened to me—and how it can happen to anyone else who "can't wait." Our intentions can be so right, but they can turn out so wrong when we move too fast without listening or getting proper instructions. Our flesh can put us into a mess!

You might be saying to yourself as you read this book, "I never wanted to be married that badly. This isn't my problem." Well, let me say this: whatever your problem is, make sure your timing is right, and follow the proper ways to get that problem solved.

If you don't follow the leading of the Lord—or whomever you've placed over your life—you will feel like you are walk into a deep ditch and wishing someone would come and get you out. Some would say that I "put the wagon before the horse," and that was just what I did. My steps were crooked too. It was like I was wearing oversized shoes with three-inch heels, walking down a broken sidewalk full of holes that needed repair, and slipping and getting stuck in every crack—all while crying for help. My life was becoming a vessel of dishonor, and I didn't even know it. How can a vessel be filled if it's cracked or broken or hidden? This was just how I felt, and it needed to change. I needed to line up with God's Word so he could put the right size shoes on me: my own size. Yes, we can sometimes get ahead of ourselves. We need to follow instructions that will get us to our hearts' desires.

"He who finds a wife finds what is good" (Proverbs 18:22).

Nobody but God can find us when we are lost and breaking. He cleans us up by teaching us his ways of doing things.

My friends and I loved to play with an imaginary family in my dollhouse. I always wanted to pretend to be the mother so I could have a marriage like my mom and dad. Like I said, I came to realize that this desire, which seemed so good, brought me down into a deep hole where I felt like an empty vessel in a crooked place.

I had always believed in and feared God, but his ordering of my steps was something I was not aware of. Never making the right choice was a bad problem for me. In fact, I didn't think that making right choices was necessary in order to have a happy, successful life. I thought that all was well in my life. After all, there wasn't anything wrong with the word *marriage*, and it was supposed to be every young girl's dream, right?

I found out the hard way that wanting anything too badly will throw a person's entire life off track. My desire wasn't what anyone would call normal. I was a child who was becoming mentally sick and unstable. However, my problem was the last thing on anyone's mind. My own mom and dad didn't know how bad it was getting, and neither did I.

Remember that anything that takes you away from the normal is unstable. I desired marriage to the point that I no longer wanted to go to school or do anything else. I sat in my classes, thinking about having a boyfriend so we could get married. I know this was a sick way of thinking. Thank God for bringing me out of that mind-set. A person doesn't have to feel ugly or unwanted to think this way.

I learned that even if things are right, the timing must be right also. I heard my parents say to us, "Don't let anyone pick the rose before it blossoms." It was their way of saying, "Before you start thinking about having a boyfriend, wait until you learn everything you need to know about some things in life. Wait until you're old enough to understand."

But I let my flesh get in my way. I said to myself, "If I get married, I will not be living in sin." I was trying to find a way to please my flesh. You see, it was never a problem for my sisters and I to meet someone; most every guy liked us. We were very pretty girls. But it was later in life when I learned how important it was that the wagon not be before the horse. I didn't think about getting to know someone and spending time learning one another's ways before choosing to marry.

In church, the teacher's main message was that there was to be no sexual relationship before marriage. I loved God and his Son, Jesus, so much that I always wanted to be obedient to God and to my parents. So when I felt the need for sexual intercourse come over me, I always wanted to get married. I always felt the need to be married so I could continue to please the Lord. Like I said, I really loved the Lord. Once I had a relationship with God, it was a done deal. I made up my mind that I would never let it go.

Some people say, "When you fall off the horse, don't just lie on the ground. Get back up, dust yourself off, and get back in the saddle." I imagine that the person who created that statement loved the Lord and the journey that had been chosen for his or her life. I didn't care how crooked my life seemed. God was always there to straighten it back out. That belief enabled me to continue my life's journey.

Let me tell you about some of the crooked places I've had in my life.

In tenth grade, my boyfriend and I had a great relationship. We communicated well at the time. All was well, I thought, but it was one of the most desperate times of my life. I still wanted to be married. I

know you've heard me say it before, but
that was just the way it was.

Some people still think this way today.
They think that they can never do anything
unless they first get married, that life
cannot go on if they are not married first.
That was what we heard coming from the
church. But they never taught us when
and how to date. If we liked anyone, we
got in trouble. If someone had a baby, the
parents had to get married. Even though
the church wanted the best for us, they
didn't talk about the subject. They just
told us what we'd better not do. During
my youth, a person would get hit in the
mouth for asking questions about sexual
intercourse.

I never knew that the flesh could be
so demanding over the Spirit of God. I
thought that because God had created us,
we could have or do anything that was
right. But this is not true. The Scripture

says in Psalm 37:4 (NLT), "Take delight in the Lord, and he will give you your heart's desires." To me, this meant that if I obeyed the Lord's commandments, I would not have sexual intercourse before marriage. He would guide my life along a straight path to the desires of my hearts without regrets.

In Psalm 23, David said, "The Lord is my Shepherd; I shall not want." He said this because he'd found out that nothing was going to work until he obeyed God's commandments to the fullest. You see, we can be our own blockers, stoppers, and Devil.

At a certain point in my life, being ill seemed normal to me. But today I know the right word for it: *unbalanced*. This feeling made me very depressed. I didn't think anyone could understand or change the way I felt, because it all felt normal to me. I began to destroy the friendship I had with my boyfriend, because the more I loved and enjoyed him, I more I kept pressuring him to get married. I could feel myself wanting to be closer to him. I started wishing I could see him every day. My boyfriend and I couldn't enjoy our friendship, because I kept telling him we had to get married in order to have more fun, because I couldn't have intercourse before marriage. This relationship didn't last long, because he believed that we needed to have intercourse in order to last long as friends. He said that if I really loved him, I would let him show me.

Well, some of us know that when we are out of order in dating, or we're in a premature relationship that is moving too fast, we don't use our common sense and will fall for words like "If you love me, then you'll show me, and you'll let me show you how much I love you." Some of us can relate to sexual intercourse as one of the "utmost" things we can do to prove our love. Marriage gives you a voice to have a "say so."

We were not married to each other, but I wanted him to love me more, so I went ahead and had intercourse with him. I thought this would make me very happy, but it didn't. However, it helped me come to my senses and realize that I needed to calm down, because, as Mom would say, "you can't move forward if you put the cart before the horse" or "why buy the cow if you can get the milk for free?," meaning that if a guy can get you in bed before marrying you, he doesn't have to marry you to get what he wants. He doesn't have to pay a price, and there is nothing else to look forward to after that.

I felt sad afterward, because I knew that this was not the right way to go. I loved him so much, but I was not aware that my need for marriage was a need for sex too—until I had intercourse with him.

I was ashamed to tell my parents what I'd done and that I was having feelings down in that area of my body. I didn't tell anyone—not even the counselors at school—about how I felt, and I received no teaching or training about sex education. Yes, I thought I was ready to be married, and I fell for my boyfriend's words, so I showed him how much I was a fool for his love.

Well, sad to say, after he found out that I was pregnant with his baby, he never hung around to prove his love for me. You see, he'd said that he loved me, but he'd never said that he would cherish me. And you don't have to wonder whether or not he married me. In fact, I thought that I would never see him again. I waited, pregnant and scared, not knowing how to let anyone know about losing my virginity. I had to tell my parents and siblings about the bad news on my own. But something good came out of it. I had a beautiful baby.

During the time I was pregnant, my sister needed a kidney transplant, and I was the perfect match out of all my siblings. At that time, no one knew I was pregnant. My sister was in terrible need of a kidney right away, and I was the perfect match. But how was I to tell them about me? I really needed God's help to make this crooked situation straight, and He did.

First, I started out by asking different people what I should do. How could I let my family know that I was pregnant? I felt like my world was coming to an end. Some people said, "Let your sister die. She's lived to be nineteen, and that's enough time for her." My sister was one year older than me. Others said, "Kill the baby and save your sister." Neither advice sounded or felt good to hear. Yes, it changed the way I felt; it made me feel worse. I wanted my baby, even though I was by myself. And I wanted my sister to live a longer, healthy life. I remember feeling very bad and crying a lot.

One day I decided to stay in my room and think and just clear my mind. Even after all of the warring in my mind about what I should do and how I should handle the situation, I never thought about asking God to help me decide what I should do to resolve this problem. James 4:2 says, "You have not because you ask not." When you pray to God, He will work out any difficult problem you have in your life.

One night while I was in my room, I was so tired of crying and feeling bad that I began to cry out to God and call on him for help. I thought about my decision, little knowing that God was in the room with me and inside of me. After releasing all of my frustrations, I just lay there quietly, feeling relaxed, and listened to a voice inside my mind say, "Have the baby, and then give your sister the kidney." Just like that, God had the answer waiting inside me.

"Don't pray like the hypocrites, for they pray out in the streets to be seen" (Matthew 6:1–4).

God did not answer me when I asked everyone else for advice. It was only when I went into my room to talk with him that he answered me. When we share our troubles with people who do not talk to God, the problems will never be given to God to solve them. We are only being comforted for a little while. We still need to pray so that God can bring us in front of the right people. We are made in the image of God, the Supreme Being. We are his vessels of honor, believing and carrying out his Word to others. When we take our problems to God in prayer, he reveals to us the right way to go. The right choice helps us get the right answer.

Let's take a look at Kish's son Saul when he met Samuel, God's prophet, the man of God. I have summarized Samuel 9 in my own words.

One day Kish's donkeys strayed away, and he told Saul, "Take a servant with you and go look for the donkeys." They passed through the hill county of Ephraim and the area of Shalisha, but they did not find them. They went looking all over, but still the donkeys were nowhere to be found. Saul said to the servant, "Let's go back. If we don't go back, my father will stop worrying about the donkeys and start worrying about us." The servant said, "Wait. There is a man of God who lives in a town near here, and he's amazing! Everything he says comes true. Let's talk to him. Maybe he can tell us where to look."

You see, Saul was praying as he was talking to the servant, and at the end of his prayer, he was given what to do. Because Saul was telling the servant about his problem, God spoke out of the mouth of the servant. We have to be around people who care about us and themselves in order to get the right answer. When we want to be blessed, God sends us to the right people. All he needs is a believer in him.

Saul asked the servant, "How can we talk to the prophet when we don't have anything to give him?" The servant had a small piece of silver. He said, "We can give him this, and then he will tell us where to look for the donkeys." So they went, being led by God, and found Samuel, who already knew they were coming.

When we are concerned about our problems and are telling them to the right person or people, we are talking to God. And God will meet us in the middle. The Supreme Being created us to help one another. While we are praying, God is talking about us to someone who can help us. Samuel, the prophet, knew that Saul and his servant were coming. They went to the town, and just as they were going through the gate, Samuel was coming out on his way to the place of worship. Saul met Samuel on the road to worship, and we will know that we are on the right road when we stay off the low road. The high road is the road to prosperity. Think about that.

Saul asked Samuel if he was the one who saw visions. Samuel said, "Yes, I am the one who sees visions." They believed the prophet and took the high road in their minds. Jesus said, "If I be lifted up in the earth, I will draw all men unto me" (John 12:32). Samuel said, "In the morning I will answer your question. And don't worry about the donkeys that ran off three days ago, for they have already been found."

We must look at God when we pray! When I was pregnant and worrying about what to do, I thought I couldn't have the baby unless I let my sister die. I had no one around me like Saul's servant, but I had my *conscience*, my inner sense, which God uses to tell us what to do. Thank God for inner awareness. I made the right choice. I didn't have to regret it.

Back then, I didn't know that God was in the room with me all the time. Now I know that he was with me even while I was out asking other people what to do. God showed me during my prayer that my boyfriend might have loved me like he said, but that he didn't cherish me. God wanted me to look at the realty of it all. If my boyfriend had really loved me, he would have not pushed me into having sex, knowing that he did not want to have children or be married and cherish me yet.

In fact, he didn't even love himself, because if he had loved himself, he would not have put himself into that mess either. I know that in his heart he felt sorry for what he put us through. Having to deny the truth doesn't make anyone feel good. I didn't go back with him, because I didn't want any more regrets. You see, God had taken me from that crooked place of regrets and had placed me in a straight path of forgiveness where I didn't feel the pain and suffering of regret. I was happy with myself and my baby. God had given me a good job and my own apartment, and I was up on my feet, with no more regrets. I forgave my boyfriend and wished him a change in life, because my life had already changed. I knew that if God could take care of me that far, he could continue to do so.

Marriage is for a lifetime. Trust me: you will have all the time in the world to have sexual intercourse after you get married. As Mama said to me, my sisters, and my friends, "If a guy loves you, he will not be in a rush," but I did not want to understand that statement at the time. My head was too full of pleasing my flesh.

Please let this statement be a blessing to you. It has now become a blessing to me and to the people I teach. I knew—and my boyfriend knew—that he was the first person I had ever been with. But right or wrong, it did not matter at that point. The situation had already occurred.

If I had kept thinking about the aspect of right or wrong, I would not have found peace during the nine years that followed. Instead, God enabled me to forgive him and enjoy all of the great blessings that were happening in my life. If I had kept thinking about how wrong things were, I would never have asked for forgiveness for the wrongs I had done. Remember, my boyfriend wasn't by himself in the wrongdoing. Whatever the problem, we all play a role, whether someone is doing us wrong or we are allowing it to happen to us.

I played the part of allowing it to happen, so I had to repent. I didn't have to say yes to sex, and he didn't make me say yes. It was my choice as well as his. When I came to this conclusion, all the hurt and pain left me, because I was no longer thinking crookedly. I was thinking straight.

2

The Way We Think Has a Lot to Do with the Way We Feel

As long as I blamed the whole problem on my boyfriend, I felt worse and worse. But God showed me that I was a character in this story. Eventually I accepted the way God revealed my situation to me. I played a big part in my own life story, and I needed to be concerned about the role I played. Scripture says not to worry about the speck in your friend's eye when you have a log in your own" (Matthew 7:3). When I understood this, God took me out of my painful situation.

We need to ask God to forgive us for being a part of any terrible situation, even if we feel like we are innocent. Somehow we have opened a door and let the terrible in. If I had never seen my situation the way God showed it to me, I would never have found the path to having no more regret. I needed to allow God to make all of my cooked places straight.

If you do what God requires you to do, you will never have to suffer any of these things or cause a child to have one parent because of wrong timing: being too young or unmarried. Then your life will be so much better. If you have already done it and don't know what to do, don't sit there and beat yourself up about the mistakes you've made. Find the role you played, and become a better character in the story so you can complete the chapter and become the hero at the end. Like I said, get up, dust yourself off, and get back in the saddle, moving forward on the journey toward achieving your dreams and the desires of your heart.

The key is to forgive everyone who may have hurt you—now or in your past. Follow my steps in this story, and God will bring you out, just as he did me, into a life with no more regrets. I hope this book will help you get on and stay on the right path, even as you say yes to God's way of doing things.

Yes, God is everywhere, and I know that he wants us to be in the right place so he can show off the beauty he's placed within us and bless us with the person who will cherish us the most. He doesn't want to see us crying and pleading with him to get us out of a troubled relationship.

God is always waiting for us to call his name, and he will come and rescue us from all of our troubles. David said in Psalm 139 that the Lord knows everything about us. He knows when we sit down and when we stand up. He knows our every thought from far away. He charts the path ahead of us and tells us where to stop and rest. Every moment, he knows where we are. He knows what we are going to say even before we say it. Yes, he does! He warns us before we make mistakes. God knows and love us so much. He makes sure our path is clear before we cross or go through it.

3

God Makes a Way for Us

God is always there to help us with all of our infirmities. Yes, God is always there for us in times of trouble, to heal us and give us joy that goes beyond happiness. Happiness is for a moment, but joy lasts forever.

God will place great people in your life, just as he has done for me. They will help you break away from your past by being great helpers and supporters and by giving you good advice.

God sent his Son, Jesus Christ, to demonstrate how we are to behave.

I have learned that God doesn't mean for us to suffer, because he loved us so much that he sent his only beloved Son to earth to teach us how to do things the right way. Jesus gave us—and still gives us—specific instructions that will lead us to our victories. But it is we ourselves who walk into bad choices. God does not make bad choices for us.

God wants to operate in us and through us. He wants us to refrain from sorrow so that we can keep joy and happiness in our lives. Isaiah 26:3 (ESV) says, You will keep him in perfect peace whose mind is stayed on you, because he trusts in you.

Here is something you should know. Moving too fast will cause you to break the foundation that God has caused you to build on. Every relationship needs a rock to stand on. Without the rock, your relationship will be sinking sand. "Therefore the Lord God says: 'Look I have laid a foundation in Zion, a tested stone, a precious cornerstone, a sure foundation, the one who believes will be unshakeable'" (Isaiah 28:16).

In Matthew 16:18, Jesus said, "Upon this rock I will build my church, and the gates of hell shall not prevail against it." Trust in the Lord with all of your problems, and He will bring you out from them!

4

Think Before You Act: Don't Put the Cart before the Horse

Don't waste time and years dreaming about what you want to do or need to do with your life but never spend any time gathering information or learning how to make it happen. David said, "Teach us how to number our days that we may gain a heart of wisdom" (Psalm 90:12).

Many times in life, we think we need to rush into things before we have what we need. We see the dream, but we never think to figure out how to make it come to pass. As for me, I was very young when I wanted a boyfriend instead of having fun with my dolls, toys, and friends. I was miserable and unhappy. I wanted people and things in my life before the right timing. I was putting the cart before the horse.

One of the first things God wants us to do as children is to listen to our parents. The apostle Paul said in Ephesian 6:1, "Children, obey your parents, for this is the will of God for you."

I believe that Paul was saying, "Children, go to school, get your education, and become creative, because God has already placed many gifts and talents on the inside of you." We are all God's children under his mighty authority.

When we desire something positive, all we need to do is write it in a journal. Taking one step at time, we should get advice from a person or people who have the authority of God over their lives, and use our dreams and visions as a road map. Then we can see and make things happen. Habakkuk 2:2(NLT) says,Then the Lord said to me: "write my answer plainly on a tablet. So that a runner can carry the correct message to others"

When I was in kindergarten, the teacher invited parents with great job careers to our class as a school project. They described their professions and told us how long it had taken them to complete school and all the requirements for becoming who they wanted to be in life. You see, they were showing us the way we should go. Ephesians 6:4 says, "Fathers, do not provoke your children to anger, but bring them up in the discipline and instruction of the lord."

I also remember taking courses in child care. I read in one of the books that children five years old and under are natural-born sponges. I realized that this was why the teacher had invited the parents to my kindergarten class. It was to help us focus on our futures and stir up the gifts and talents that were inside us. They were instilling in us the chance to start an early process of learning so we could be productive on the earth. Then the teacher asked us what or who we wanted to be in life. They were focused on bringing out the best in us. This is why we should not despise teachers. They are here to keep us in the will of God by keeping us focused on being creative and productive like our Father in heaven.

5

We Are Natural-Born Creators

When we were born into this world, we were born to be creators and not destroyers. We can either destroy the earth or be productive on the earth. It starts when we are born.

Now I understand that my mother and father chastising me was the right thing. It was to keep my mind focused on having a good life, finishing school, not going too fast in life, and walking at the right pace.

One day I asked a group of young children, ages two through eighteen, what was on their minds at that moment. I wanted to teach them that when they dreamed, they needed to believe in the dream and live the life that would help them make that dream come true. I asked everyone what was on their hearts at that moment. Some said they wanted to have sexual intercourse more than anything else in this world, and they knew that desire was destroying what they really wanted to become in the future. In fact, most of them were wrestling with two desires: a desire to obey their parents and a desire to have sexual intercourse.

One of the kids said he was having such uncontrollable feelings that they were giving him terrible headaches and causing him to fight with his parents and not get along with anyone in the house. This same kid wanted to be a basketball star in the future. This worried him because every time he was ready to play ball, he couldn't get along with his teachers, coaches, or teammates—just like the situation at home. He had sex on his mind all day, and this was why he did not have a normal life. In class, he wasn't able to focus on his work, and the teachers called his mom to report his failing grades. They really needed to find out what was going on with him, but no one in his family knew what was wrong. So they all began to label him as "mean and hateful." He began to see himself as a cool kid who just needed a girlfriend to become focused.

I thank God that I was able to let him know what was causing this effect. I was able to tell him that he was wrestling with his flesh, and that was the frustration. I told him that I was a counselor of God who could help him win his battle, with the help of God. I told him that his timing was wrong and was stopping him from growing toward his career, that it was normal to have those feelings, and that he had the power to control them.

I said that there was a time and season for everything, but it was not his time and season yet. If he accepted what I was saying to him, things would go a lot smoother for him. I said that he needed to put his desire for sex on the back burner, do what he was told to do, obey those in authority over him, and play basketball. Basketball was acceptable for his age— in heaven and on earth. I told him not to think that he could never have a sexual relationship, but I warned him that if he did it now, it would destroy his future career and relationship with a wife. And this goes for any of us who do something before the right time and season.

I told this boy that he was stuck because he was dwelling on something that could be a good idea in the future but would cause him problems in this time and season. You see, having sex out of season takes the beauty out of the relationship. I told him that God wanted to make the crooked places straight in his life. The boy said he had never heard anyone say those words before.

I got my Bible and read Isaiah 45:2 to him: "This is what the Lord says: 'I will go before you and make crooked places straight; I will break in pieces the gate of brass, and cut in sunder the bars of iron.'" When I finished reading this to him, he quickly agreed to the message of the verse and was willing to change the way he was thinking.

So, God took the crooked places in his life and made them straight. The young boy was happy and excited, knowing that he could enjoy his life now and in the future. I told him he needed to listen to his elders so he could make it to a place in his life to experience both his desires.

He was excited to learn that everything he desired was a vision that he needed to write down and make plain, and though it tarried, he was to wait on it. "Then the Lord said to me, 'Write my answer in large clear letters on a tablet so that a

runner can read it and tell everyone else'"
(Habakkuk 2:2).

Do you see why you should wait on
the Lord? The young boy realized that he
wasn't mean and hateful. He just didn't
know what was happening to him. We
need to bring our flesh under subjection
so that we can move forward toward our
dreams. After I told this to the young man,
he said he would wait, because he was
really sincere about his career. He chose
to put the flesh under subjection until the
proper time. He was just moving too fast.
I thank God that I was able to help him
place the horse back in front of the cart.

This boy's life had gone downhill to
the point where he was depressed. He
never smiled. You would have thought he
had no teeth.

You might be feeing the same way. Maybe there's something in your life that you know you are supposed to be doing at this time, but you keep putting it on hold because the flesh is hollering out louder than your career: "Take care of me first!"

You may be feeling so miserable that you can't get along with others at the job, and at home you do the same. Your spouse, children, family, and friends want to know what is wrong with you. Why you are so isolated, discouraged, and depressed?

Well, now you know to put the flesh under subjection, because the time is not right for you now. I have heard people say that the flesh is a mess, and I have also heard that we can never please the flesh. Let me say something to you: God has given us power and authority to put the flesh under subjection. Our flesh is to be subject to the mind. The mind has authority over the flesh. Our flesh is like a physical "cart" and our mind is the "horse." The horse has the authority to pull the cart where it wants to take it, to go from point A to point Z.

The flesh doesn't have to be a mess. Having the wrong desires is what causes the flesh to be a mess. If we will separate the right thoughts from the bad thoughts, dump the bad thoughts out of the cart (which is the body), and put our desires in the right order, then we will see that the flesh is needed also in this life. God created us as flesh to help support this universe. He never made a mistake when he added flesh in his creation. We just have to know how to utilize it. I believe that he created us as flesh to help us get where we need to go. The wrong desires cause us to feel that the flesh is a mess. *We will never please the flesh until we become what God intends for us to be in life.* And then we will experience great blessings in our bodies.

Your flesh has a lot to do with your feelings of healing, joy, rest, love, and peace. But you can never reach those feelings by making bad decisions and having wrong desires.

We can seek to live healthy, pain-free lives. But we come to a place in our minds where the flesh needs peace too. I know that we are spirit and soul, but what about the instrument that holds them? The body is the flesh, and if it is such a mess, why do we fight so hard to live in it and keep it alive?

Whatever your age, I hope you can benefit from this story. You can overpower the Enemy in your mind—in the way you think—even when it tries to come between you and your life's dreams.

6

Recognizing My Angels

The angels that God sends look like you and me. When you see angels, you have to be able to identify them. God sends them to supply your needs. Know your own needs so they can move on your behalf. Angels don't show up for nothing. That's why the Scripture says, "Don't forget to show hospitality to strangers. By so doing, some people have shown hospitality to angels without knowing it" (Hebrews 13:12).

God sends angels to assist us when we are in need of natural or supernatural assistance. When you are not aware of your angels, they can't work for you. The angels can only work for you if you acknowledge your need and acknowledge that they come to supply your need on

God's behalf. Stop trying every other way, and start praying. Tell God all your business, just as you tell your friends and family. Wait and rely on the response he gives you. Then, before you know it, he will assign angels to go to work for you. Proverbs 3:6 says, "In all your ways acknowledge him, and he shall direct your paths."

Give God the praise, and rejoice in knowing that he doesn't make mistakes like we do. God is the one who does great things for us. This doesn't mean that we can't give thanks to those on earth, but we must thank him first, recognizing that he is the one who is causing a positive effect. Without God, the leader and ruler of authority, there would be no positive manifestation. God places in the angels his messages and power to help us.

7
God's Divine Timing

I was led by the Lord to move to Georgia at the age of thirty-six. After about six months there, I was sitting on the couch in my house when someone knocked at my backdoor. It was a stranger, a man whom I had never seen before. He had a sweet, sweet approach. He said to me, "Ma'am, you don't know me, and I don't know you, but the Lord told me to tell you that you have something serious going on in your body, and you need to go to the doctor to see about it. It is either major or minor, but you have a problem going on in your body." He couldn't tell me exactly where it was, but all he knew was that I had a problem going on in my body.

I realize now that sometimes God doesn't tell his messengers everything but just gives them enough to help us get started on the road. For me, it involved getting a physical exam and not doing things on my own. This was the right road to God's glory and my healing. I knew that God had sent this man, for now my situation made sense. Only a few days prior I had done a breast exam on myself, and I knew the man's visit wasn't just a coincidence.

I started thanking God for sending the man to me. Then I prayed, "Lord, show me where the problem is." I asked him to guide me. If I had not prayed, I would have been confused, and God does not operate in a state of confusion. This was a supernatural experience. What stranger knocks on someone's door to tell her something like this? The man didn't ask for any money; he just told me what I needed to know and then left in peace. He was my angel of message.

If I'd had the faith back then that I have today, I would have prayed for God to remove the problem from my body. But I thank God today for this experience. Now I can help you and others gain the faith that I have and more.

A few days after I prayed, the pain got greater, and I went to the doctor. I told him where I was hurting. The doctor examined my breast. During this time, I was traveling and singing at different places and churches, and I had an engagement on that following Saturday. My doctor told me I shouldn't go out of town but stay to get a biopsy.

When I got the news that I had stage four breast cancer, I started crying. It scared me, as it would scare anyone to hear that she has the big C-word. I prayed to God and said, "Lord, I don't know anyone in the city who can tell me where to go from here." As soon as I said those words, a nurse walked in. All the doctors had just come in, given me the news, and walked out. The nurse came in right after I'd received the news. She was my angel to guide me.

She came in wearing a white dress and nurse's cap. I remember saying, "She doesn't look like a modern-day nurse. She's dressed like the nurses of old." She had blonde hair and the warmth of a mother who comes when you hurt yourself. She had the wisdom of a grandmother. She walked up to me, hugged me, and told me that she wanted to help me get across the street to see the other doctor. I was still in a shock. She told me not to give up the fight, to keep believing in God, no matter what I heard.

The Scripture says, "The battle is not mine; it is the Lord's." And the nurse said, "The battle is not yours but the Lord's. If you keep the faith and look to God through your doctors and obey your doctors, you will win the fight. Don't give up. This is the season when God is making all the crooked places straight in your life." She told me that her mom had beaten cancer and that I could do the same thing. We got across the street, and I hugged her. When I was ready to say thank you, she wasn't there anymore. I knew then that she was another one of my guardian angels that God had sent to encourage me.

A week later, I met another doctor who told me that the cancer was stage four and that I should have surgery right away to remove it. He told me the story of one of his former patients, a twenty-four-year-old woman with two children, who had said to him in a very nasty way, "You can't remove my cancer. God is going to remove my cancer." That woman had never had enough of a prayer life to know the truth.

How can we say that someone is not telling the truth if we don't pray to get the answer from God? When we pray to God, he directs our path, letting us know whom to believe and rely on. We can't say whether someone is lying or telling the truth without a prayer life.

As the doctor was talking, all I could hear God say was, "The kinder you are, the better you can hear." I stayed calm. I did not denounce the doctor's career or insult him. I believed in the doctor. If Jesus had been against the opinions of doctors, he would not have positioned Luke as one of his disciples. I believe that doctors are just as happy as we are when God gives us a divine healing. They are not our enemies; they are reporters and helpers. I could hear the Lord say amen in response to my thoughts.

I repeated the Lord's amen. The doctor looked at me, and his compassion grew.

His compassion grew even greater after I agreed with him. By agreeing with God and seeking the doctor's help, God gave the doctor more compassion for me, which made him want to help me even more. Everybody needs a helping hand, and doctors are here to lend us one. Doctors are supporters of the universe.

Some Christians think that God doesn't operate through doctors and that doctors are of the Devil. These people believe they can go on saying, "Hallelujah, thank you, Jesus. I don't have cancer" (or whatever they've gone to the doctor for). Remember that we are the ones who go to the doctors. The doctors don't know our condition until we go to the hospital. Why do people go for help and then not want to be told what to do? It's the same with church; people go to church, but they don't want the preacher to tell them what to do. All we're doing is telling ourselves lies. Doctors tell the truth, but what they say doesn't have to be the fact.

When one doctor gives you bad news, and you go and get a second opinion, and that doctor gives you good news, don't say, "Ha! That other doctor lied." Instead, why don't you say, "God intervened and turned it around." Give God the recognition. Don't focus on the bad news one doctor gave you. Focus on how God took that bad news and turned things around. Doctors can only report what they see. God is the divine healer.

You cannot speak with the authority of God if you are not operating under God's authority, meaning that you can't say, "I am not sick," if you're not taking care of your body. I knew that I was not taking care of my body the way I should. That was why I couldn't have the power and authority to say that the doctor was a liar. But I was able to pray to see if I should agree with him.

God shows us whether to agree or not. We can't rebuke anyone when we are not in control of anything. How can you say that somebody is a liar if you haven't seen the truth yourself? Remember, if you're not feeling good, don't say that you are. After Jesus healed ten men of leprosy, he sent them to the priest to get a report to prove that they were healed. Only one man came back to Jesus to say thank you. God shows his proof that he is God through the doctor's report, and I say, "Thank you, Jesus." You can say you're not sick or crazy or that you have no cancer, but only if you are working toward making yourself better by walking in the "I am." You can't just live any way you want and have the faith of Christ.

The doctor said to me, "You are going to live and not die. We're going to see to that." He told me to go home, and he said that they would give me the date to have the surgery. After the surgery, about six weeks later, all was well. The cancer was gone, removed, and I was free it.

Everyone thinks that doctors are going to give us bad news, but just as God reveals bad news through doctors, he can heal us through doctors. God is the one who turns situations around. Doctors are just doing their jobs. They all work hand in hand. I was led by the Lord to follow the doctor's orders, and since then, I have been free of cancer for fourteen years. Thanks be to God!

8

The Seed

When you sow seeds to any ministry, you have to be sincere about why you are sowing it. God has prophets or servants of the Lord already in their places, waiting to sow into your life even before you meet them. They can give you the words the Lord has for your life.

Before you sow your seed, you must be focused on the issues in all sincerity. You must see clearly that there is something wrong and admit the truth to yourself: that you have tried everything to work things out but you just couldn't solve the problem. Know that no one can work anything out without help from others.

I've heard some people say that not everyone you meet is going to stay in your life anyway. Whether people bless you or hurt you, you can take a bad situation and find the good in it.

9

We Need One Another

We need the people who hurt us for a season, for we can gain wisdom and great success. If it hadn't been for the Lord in my life, I believe that I would have given up a long time ago. People hated me for whatever reason, but when they laughed and talked about me, God gave me a way to fix my flaws. People lied about me, picked on me, rejected me, tricked me, and led me on. But I stopped focusing on what they did to me and began to work on the areas that they saw as flaws in my life.

Do not spend time regretting that these kinds of people show up in your life. These are the people who make you flawless. They come around to move you to the next level in your life, bringing you closer and closer to a beautiful outcome, even if that's not what they intended.

10

Desire + Desire = Change

We can't make other people change their lives, no matter how much we want them to. They have to want change for themselves.

As long as we keep getting on them, we're just being distracted from what we're supposed to be doing for ourselves: making our lives better. Your prayers will help, but your worrying won't. You are the person you need to be concerned about.

Multiple people have to want the same thing before God can work things out among them. Matthew 18:20 says, "For where two or three gather in my name, there am I with them."

Two people can be good friends and really like each other, but one might want the other to fall in love with him or her. So that person goes to a prophet or a man or woman of God or asks God to touch the other person's mind and make that person return that same love. *God will not do a such thing.* We cannot be in love alone. It takes two who desire the same thing. Then we will see a change.

11

When Opportunity Knocks

Your problems are great tools to use for your journey. When your troubles come knocking on your heart's door, see them as great opportunities and ways to reach your goals. "For God hath not given us the spirit of fear; but of power, and of love, and of a sound mind" (2 Timothy 1:7).

Say this prayer with me three times: "Lord, I thank you, for you have nothing to do with the spirit of fear. Why should I be afraid?" Now, watch God change your fears to great opportunities!

Let's take a look at the words from that Scripture verse: "but of power, and of love, and of a sound mind."

"But of Power"

In Matthew 10:1, Jesus called his twelve disciples to him and gave them authority to drive out impure spirits and to heal every disease and sickness. As long as we have breath in us, we have the power to create. We can take the spirit of fear and create some favorable times and moments to plan our goals for achievement. We should see fear as a sign that something is wrong and that we do not have freedom. But when we quote the words "but of power," we are free to have freedom. Say this word three times with me: freedom, freedom, freedom! Now, watch the freedom of God take place in and around your life.

Remember that we were created to be like God and to increase, develop, and keep up with his creation. Genesis 1:1 says, "In the beginning God created the heavens and the earth." Think about the phrase "God created," and understand that God created us to act like him. "So God created man in his own image, in the image of God created he him; male and female created he them (Genesis 1:27). Verse 28 says that we have God's blessing to increase, develop, and maintain the good of everything he created and that we create.

"And of Love"

"For God so loved the world that he gave his only begotten son, that whosoever believeth in him should not perish but have everlasting life" (John 3:16).

When we love someone, that person's happiness means a lot to us. God placed love inside of us so that we can be protected from the spirit of fear. God

gave us the power to love ourselves as well as others, but it is very difficult to love others when we are not happy with our own lives and don't have respect for other people. Love doesn't wish for other people's possessions. Love doesn't steal. And love doesn't wish that people would die for not loving them back or engaging in a sexual relationship with them.

I've heard many people say that lust is so close to love that we can hardly tell the difference. You might have heard the same thing. If you believe this, you'd better watch out!

Long ago, I thought that even if someone didn't want me to love or like them, I had the right to love them as much as I wanted to. I thought this because John 13:34 says, "My command is this: Love each other as I love you." That was why it took me so long to get over all of the broken and bad relationships in my life. At that time, no one could have told me that I was not in the will of God. I did not have the right understanding of God's Word. Sad to say, I learned the truth the hard way from my own painful experiences. Love has its proper place in respect.

In order to have a good and healthy love life, two people have to agree to go to the next page or chapter in life. This goes for people who are either married or single. Falling in love is like a book that has many chapters in it. Two people must agree to keep turning to the next page.

First you read or look at the cover. If you think you like it, then you read the first page or chapter. If you don't want to read any further, then you close the book. If you like what you're reading, you might like to keep on going and finish.

Love is a peacemaker, not a peace-breaker. "Blessed are the peacemakers, for they will be called the children of God" (Matthew 5:9).

The name of Jesus Christ speaks for itself. God demonstrated his love to us by sending his only Son to show us how to continue doing well, even in the darkest and toughest moments of our lives. He showed us how to demonstrate true love toward one other. Jesus never saw himself as a victim. He saw that his purpose was to be the Savior of the world" (Isaiah: 53:4). He suffered and endured great pain for us.

"And of a Sound Mind"

"Let this mind be in you, which was also in Christ Jesus" (Philippians 2:5).

Have you ever heard the saying, "You are what you eat"? Well, I say, "You become what you keep thinking about." Our minds are like computers. They can store up information as long as we allow it. There were times in my life when I held on to things that hurt me so badly that it seemed as though I'd never get over them. The hurt was so bad that I just knew I was going to die.

I was diagnosed with cancer twice, and while I was on chemo and radiation, my eighteen-year-old son got killed in a crowd coming home from school. I've always said that I would never wish that much pain on my worst enemies. Have you ever felt like that? I hope you have never gotten to that place. David said, "I cried to the Lord, and he heard my cry" (Psalm 18:6).

God promised that he would not put more on me than I could bear (1

Corinthians 10:13). Come on. Say this with me three times: "But God! But God! But God!"

God turned things around in my mind. He showed me how to see things the right way and how to overcome it all. Don't look to the left or to the right. Don't go backward. Just keep moving forward! "Let God arise. Let his enemies be scattered: let them also that hate him flee before him" (Psalm 68:1). Notice the phrase "flee before him."

One day while walking in the park, I began talking to God. I said, "God, you said to me, 'Don't look to the left or to the right, and don't look back.' You said you want me to keep moving forward, and I am doing what you say. But what if my enemies—people or problems—are constantly in my face?" He said to me, "When problems appear in your goals or in people, even while you are doing well by me, believe and obey and keep all of my commandments. The problems are only a sign that you are very close to seeing your promise come to pass."

Keep your eyes on the prize, because you are getting ready to enter into your breakthrough. Keep on doing well, and see your problems as opportunities, strength, and ways to help you achieve your goals.

12

Stepping Stones

When God told me to see my problems as opportunities, I quickly saw stepping stones, a line of stones in shallow water. David said in Psalm 23:4, "Even though I walk through the valley of the shadow of death, I fear no evil: for you are with me; your rod and your staff, they comfort me."

In order to get to your purpose in life and achieve all of your hopes and dreams, you will have to walk through your valley of the shadow of death at some point.

13

Stones

You should never let anyone or anything turn your heart into stone as you walk through your valley.

I have thought about the times when I was hurt by friends and by the men whom I thought truly loved and cared for me. They smiled and ate with me and told me they loved me. But they only wanted the worst for me. Let's just say that they were very deceitful. When I found out the truth, the pain was so great that I felt a lump in my throat.

Have you ever been hurt so badly that some part of your body was in pain and it felt like it would never go away? I carried this kind of pain until other problems started occurring in my life.

It started with my health. I remember crying all day and night, and this just increased the pain that wouldn't go away. Then came the unthinkable: cancer. Who would have thought it possible?

When you hold on to the things people do that hurt you badly, it won't be long before you get sick. You've already read my story about having cancer.

One day I got so tired of the pain that I began to cry out to the Lord for help. I said, "Lord God, please take this pain away. My throat hurts so badly. Please come in and heal me."

As I was waiting in prayer, he said to me, "I can't come in, because you have a blockage in your throat. It has been there so long that it's becoming hard like bone. I did not place it inside you, and until you forgive everyone that has hurt you, I can't come inside you to heal you."

Until God spoke to me, I did not know that the pain in my throat was turning my heart to stone. You see, I was so mad and upset that I didn't know that my failure to forgive others was blocking God and locking him out.

Don't lock God out! When you are angry because of something someone has done to you, you're locking God out. When he tells you what to do, you can do it. By his Son, Jesus Christ, we are healed.

When he said that I needed to forgive everyone who had hurt me, I knew that he had graced me with the power to forgive. God will never tell us to do something we can't do. "There hath no temptation taken hold of you but such as is common to man. But God is faithful; he will not suffer you to be tempted beyond that which ye are able to bear, but with the temptation will also make a way to escape, that ye may be able to bear it (1 Corinthians 10:13).

That was when my mind changed. I realized that I had the power to forgive. And you do too.

14

Be the Seed That Fell on Good Ground

Luke 8:15 says that some seeds fall on good ground. These seeds are like people who hear the Word and remember it. Their hearts are honest and good. These people keep on believing, and much good comes from them.

There were times in my life when I worried about everything and especially about my tomorrow. Even when I had things and people in my life, they didn't seem to be enough. Everything could be going well, but I expected the worst to come. I couldn't wait for anything, and I couldn't believe anyone, including my own choices.

If I had a job, I worried about losing it. It was the same with money; I always worried that I might not have any. If I had a boyfriend, I worried that he might stop liking me. I couldn't sleep because I was worried that something bad would happen to me or to my friends or family. The cares of life were slowing me down from my true purpose. I was the seed that had fallen among thorns, even though the Lord God and my mother, father, pastor, sisters, brothers, family, and friends told me that everything would be all right.

Luke 8:14 says that the seed that falls among thorns stands for those who hear, but as those people go on their way, they are choked by life's worries, riches, and pleasures, and they do not mature.

When we worry, it only keep us from completing the things that we wish to enjoy in life—people, places, and things that you and I dream about. Worrying stops us from seeing hopes and dreams come to pass. Worrying about people or things takes way our energy, and if we have no energy, we can only wish and hope for the things we desire.

When God created everything, he didn't worry about how he was going to do it or what it would take to do it. The Bible says that he rested afterward, and no one can rest while worrying.

15

We Are the Seed

"So the word became human and made his home among us. He was full of unfailing love and faithfulness. And we have seen his glory, the glory of the Father's one and only Son" (John 1:14).

God created us and gave us the power to make right choices. Yes, he knows we are going to make mistakes, but he did not create us to make them. It just wasn't in his plan.

God sent his Son, Jesus, who was and is the Word, to demonstrate to us how to become the Word of God (the seed) so that much good can come to us.

16

Misery Loves Company

I've always heard people say, "Misery loves company." This means that people who are very unhappy want you to join them. This can come true if you allow it, but remember that spoken words are very powerful. When God created us, he gave us the power to choose. Trust me when I say that misery is not one of his choices.

Misery is not a person; it is a word that can be avoided.

After many situations occurred in my own life and in the lives of others, I began to appreciate wisdom and knowledge from my father, mother, and other leaders in authority. I learned how to recognize whether a person was suffering for goodness's sake or just from being hardheaded and rebellious.

James 1:4 says, "But let patience have its perfect work, that you may be perfect and complete, lacking nothing."

Whenever a situation in my life became too much for me to handle, I always found a substitute for it, which ended up making things worse. I wanted God to fix things *right now*, which took me back to people, places, things, and thoughts that made me even more miserable. I was not paying attention to the Scripture that says, "My brethren, count it all joy when you fall into divers temptation; knowing this, that the trying of your faith worketh patience" (James 1:2–3).

I never like to feel pain, and I know you don't as well. But pain lets you know when something is going wrong. If you pay attention to it, you can get the information you need to get turned round.

When we pray to God, he will put someone in our heart or on our mind whom we can seek out for the advice we need. Or he himself will tell us what to do. God does this so that our situation can be altered.

Some people are unhappy because they've caused their own negative effects.

I never thought to ask what was really wrong in anyone's life. I was just so ready to help make things right with the help of the Lord.

I remember a pastor saying to me, "Stop trying to help everyone else, and help yourself." Like a mother, she was afraid that someone was going to hurt me. Have you ever been hurt by the very people you're trying help?

I have learned that some people don't want your help. They're just looking for someone to join them in their misery by talking about their troubles all the time. They are not willing to listen to anyone. They would rather stay in the troubles that they've allowed to escalate in their lives.

17

Put Away the Past

Sometimes trouble comes, and situations in life seem too hard to bear. But you won't go back to Egypt. You will continue to follow your dreams and have a great outcome. Here are the testimonies of some people who have overcome their difficulties.

When I first met Prophetess Horn, I really did not fully understand what was going to take place in my life—not just for myself but for my family as well. As a full adult, I found myself lost in my mind, full of anger, very selfish, and extremely childish. To be honest, my life was heading down the road to destruction. I thought that chasing worldly "things" would fix all my issues. I realized through this ministry that my mind-set was wrong. My entire family was in need of major help, help that could only come through God using Prophetess Horn as a vessel. My marriage was very fragile, and every relationship in my life was either broken or out of place.

Her teaching has set my life on the right track. For years God has blessed me over and over through Liberty Without Walls Ministries Inc., not just in the form of money or jobs but in even more important things. God has blessed me through her teaching to have a stable mind and maturity and to finally have my life in the proper order. God has especially blessed my marriage with a new and stronger foundation. The renewal of our wedding vows will take place on March 28, 2015. Now, that is God's working! I thank God for this ministry, and I know that this book will not only be a blessing to me but to many, many others as well. Thank you so much, Prophetess Horn

—*Kurtina Moore*

There was a time in my life when I lived with many regrets. Since I met Prophetess Horn, I now live a life without regrets. I once felt overwhelmed and could not make the right choices in life's situations. I have since learned how to let go of things I cannot change and leave them alone. I learned to let go of heartache and pain. My pain was severe, as I did not know how to let go of a bad relationship. I can truly say that the words taught through Prophetess Horn have set me free. God has really anointed her to break the chains that have weighed me down. I know that the words in this book will be a blessing to everyone and will break every chain in Jesus's name.

Patricia Perry

I have known Prophetess Horn since we were teenagers. She always loved to help lead people in the right direction and draw them close to God. As time went by in my life, things didn't work out as

I'd planned. Prophetess Horn came and spoke into my life, and through her, God made my crooked places straight. I was in need of a job and a place to stay, and God came through for me through Prophetess Horn on my behalf. No matter what I have gone through, she has always been there to help me overcome it. She is currently teaching me how to live a life without regrets. Thank you, Prophetess Horn.

—Sheila Talton

To learn more about me and my ministry, you can visit the website at *www.libertywithoutwallsministries.us*. My itinerary and other information are available, along with access to PayPal, where donation, contributions, and seed-sowing are available. You can also send your prayer requests by clicking the email icon on the left of the screen.

About the Book

Isaiah 26:7 (CEV) says, "Our Lord, you always do right, and you make the path smooth for those who obey you."

This book is written for those who are sick and tired of living lives full of regret. You can have a complete turnaround in your life by reading this book and following the steps that God has for you to take. God can take you out of a dark path or dilemma that you have created and bring you into a life of success through the leading of his Word. God wants to change the way you think so that you can have everything he promised to give you. Everything that is written in his Word shall come to pass. God's word is so true! We just need to believe in him and hear the "I am" in our thoughts, which was the way he identified himself to Moses: "'But what should I say, if they ask me your name?' God said to

Moses: I am the eternal God. So tell them that the Lord, whose name is 'I Am,' has sent you" (Exodus 3:13b–14 CEV).

If you believe what the Scripture says, you can change all of the crooked places in your life in an instant. You see, God never intended for us to make more mistakes and have less success. He will be whatever and whoever you want and need him to be. God wants us to have greater successes and fewer regrets. This book contains several stories about my life and how God took bad situations (negative) and became the "I Am" in my life (positive), blessing me to a place of good health, wealth, and prosperity.